Using Freelance Platforms Safely and Effectively

BY

WES COWLEY

THE-EFA.ORG

Copyright © 2021 Wes Cowley
Cover and design © 2021 Editorial Freelancers Association
New York, NY

All rights reserved.
No part of this publication may be reproduced, distributed, or transmitted in any form or by any means, including, but not limited to, photocopying, recording, or other electronic or mechanical methods, without the prior written permission of the publisher, except in the case of brief quotations embodied in critical reviews and certain other noncommercial uses permitted by copyright law. For permission requests, write to the publisher at "Attention: Publications Chairperson," at the address below.

266 West 37th St. 20th Floor
New York, NY 10018
office@the-efa.org

ISBN paperback 978-1-880407-48-6
ISBN ebook 978-1-880407-49-3

Cowley, Wes. *Using Freelance Platforms Safely and Effectively.*
Published in the United States of America by the Editorial Freelancers Association.

BISAC Subject Categories:| Business & Economics/Freelance & Self-Employment | Business & Economics/Careers/Job Hunting | Business & Economics/E-commerce/small business

Legal Disclaimer
While the publisher and author have made every attempt to verify that the information provided in this book is correct and up to date, the publisher and author assume no responsibility for any error, inaccuracy, or omission. The advice, examples, and strategies contained herein are not suitable for every situation. Neither the publisher nor author shall be liable for damages arising therefrom. This book is not intended for use as a source of legal or financial advice. Running a business involves complex legal and financial issues. You should always retain competent legal and financial professionals to provide guidance.

EFA Publications Director: Robin Martin
Copyeditor: Nanette Day
Proofreader: Erin Roll
Book Designer: Kevin Callahan | BNGO Books
Cover Designer: Ann Marie Manca

See more by the author:
Web: wordsbywes.ink

Contents

1. Introduction	1
2. Overview of the Platforms	5
Terms	5
Types of platforms	5
Pros and cons	6
How do you choose?	9
3. Understanding How a Platform Works	11
What kind of communication is allowed?	11
What are the exclusivity rules?	12
How do you bid on a job?	12
What types of pricing models are supported?	13
What are the fee structures?	13
How do you get a contract?	15
How do you get paid?	15
How do the freelancer ratings work?	16
What is the dispute process?	17
Summary	17
4. Establishing and Managing Your Reputation	19
5. Setting Rates	21
6. Vetting Clients and Their Material	23
7. Avoiding Scams	25

8. Parting Words	29
References	31
General	31
Fiverr	31
Freelancer.com	33
Guru	34
PeoplePerHour	36
Reedsy	37
Upwork	38

1. Introduction

Freelance platforms such as Upwork, Freelancer.com,[1] Reedsy, and Fiverr have mixed reputations among the publishing community and the wider freelance world. Some people find them a quagmire of scams and low-paying jobs; others see a lucrative source of work and a way to establish or expand their client base. There's truth in both perspectives.

One only needs to browse the platforms' forums to see that many people, both freelancers and clients, have become victims of scams, with more falling for the traps every day. There are also clients who offer what, to established professionals, are insultingly low rates in order to exploit some freelancers' desperation. Scams and problem clients aren't specific to platforms, but with millions of users, the sites' scale magnifies and concentrates the problems.

Yet many freelancers have built successful, well-paying careers exclusively using freelance platforms; others have kick-started or augmented careers with clients both on and off the sites. The path to success and safety requires becoming informed before jumping in, and continually using caution and applying common sense.

I started freelance editing in 2019 after retiring from a long career in information technology. At the time, I didn't really know how to start finding clients, but I knew some people were making good money using Fiverr. I researched several of the major (and not-so-major) freelance

---

1. To avoid confusion, I use ".com" after Freelancer to refer to the platform with that name.

platforms and decided to try Upwork.[2] Using that platform, I've worked with about 125 clients from all over the world—individuals, small businesses, Fortune 500 companies, and academic institutions—and I've recently started diversifying to a growing network of clients off the platform. I saw many horror stories during my initial research (and I still do), but I also saw that most of those were easily avoidable. What I'm sharing here is a combination of things I learned during that research that kept me away from the common pitfalls, and some things I wish I knew when I started.

This booklet highlights things to consider when starting to use freelance platforms. It covers aspects you, as an editorial freelancer, should know in order to effectively use the sites. I won't go into all the details of how each platform works—there's not enough space for that, and, more importantly, the details change often. Rather, I'll summarize the things to pay attention to, such as the rules, the proposal and contract processes, and the rate structures. I'll also talk about managing your reputation and vetting clients and their material. Finally, I'll cover some of the ways freelancers can be scammed and how to avoid those traps.

Some examples are specific to editorial freelancers, the target audience for this booklet. But the booklet is general enough that freelancers in other fields may benefit as well. The examples pull more heavily from Upwork than the other platforms for two reasons: It leads in size, popularity, and breadth of services at the time of this writing,[3] and I began my freelance career as a user of this platform. However, this booklet

---

2. I won't go into why I chose Upwork over the others, as my criteria and dealbreakers may not be the same as yours. There are downsides to all of the platforms, which I'll get into later. To me, Upwork looked like the least bad option, and it has worked out very well. Other platforms may make more sense to you.

3. Comparable statistics are not available from the platforms across all metrics. The following numbers are from the platforms' sites, including job and freelancer search results, and investor disclosures as of this writing. *Active job posts*: Upwork, 213K; Freelancer.com, 16K; Guru, 2.3K; PeoplePerHour, 3.6K. *Clients purchasing services within the last 12 months*: Upwork, >600K; Fiverr, 3.8M. *Freelancers*: Freelancer.com, 2M; Reedsy, 2.5K; Guru, 1.8M. *Registered users (possibly including inactive)*: Freelancer, 51M; Reedsy, 1M; Guru, 800K; PeoplePerHour, 1.2M (clients only).

does contain examples from other platforms and general best practices that can apply to most, if not all, of them. My focus is on giving you information to successfully and safely integrate freelance platforms into your business.

2. Overview of the Platforms

Terms

I use a few key terms consistently: A **client** is someone who engages a **freelancer** in a **contract** to complete a **project** (e.g., editing a book, formatting a paper, etc.). Some platforms use different terms; Fiverr, for example, uses "buyer" for clients and "seller" for freelancers. To avoid confusion, I use "client" and "freelancer" consistently. The **freelance platform** (or just **platform**) is an intermediary in the transaction, providing means and support for freelancers and clients to connect, communicate, and complete their contract. In most cases, clients and freelancers do not need to buy a **subscription** to the platform, but these are usually available and come with extra features and perks. The platforms make most of their money by charging **fees** that are a percentage of the client's payment to the freelancer.

Types of platforms

There are many freelance-related platforms and several different business models for the sites and for the freelancer. Here, I focus on three models in which the platform is significantly involved in the freelancer–client relationship by facilitating communication and managing payments. Some of the platforms support two or all three models.

Job boards: Clients post ads describing the work they need done. Freelancers search the job list and apply to ads matching their skills. Examples: Upwork, Freelancer.com, Guru, PeoplePerHour, and Fiverr.

Freelancer directories: Freelancers post profiles describing their services. Clients search those for people meeting their needs, contact candidates to discuss the project, and hire one or more of them. Examples: Reedsy, Upwork, Freelancer.com, Guru, and PeoplePerHour.

Project (or gig) boards: Freelancers post ads offering packaged projects with defined scopes, terms, and delivery times. For example, an ad might offer light editing of 1,000 words in seven days for $30. Project ads often include options for different scope levels or add-ons. Clients browse those projects, choose one that meets their needs, and order the package from the freelancer. Fiverr made this model famous, and other platforms, including Upwork, Freelancer.com, and PeoplePerHour, have since added it to their offerings.

I focus on six platforms here: Upwork, Freelancer.com, Guru, Reedsy, Fiverr, and PeoplePerHour. There are many others, but these are representative of the types of platforms currently available. I left out traditional job boards (e.g., Craigslist, Mediabistro, and the EFA's Job List), which have no involvement in the contracts. I also don't talk about referral services, like LinkedIn ProFinder,[4] which match clients to freelancers, but otherwise stay out of the transaction.

Pros and cons

Should you use one of the freelance platforms? That's a business—and personal—choice, and there are pros and cons to consider.

---

4. LinkedIn's freelancer model seems to be changing; as of this writing, it's not clear how it will evolve.

USING FREELANCE PLATFORMS SAFELY AND EFFECTIVELY

Pros

You may find a reduced need for other marketing. Once you add your freelancer profile to one of the platforms, it's visible to clients on the site and sometimes on search engines like Google. As your reputation on the platform grows, you stand out more to clients. Some platforms suggest successful freelancers to clients and promote them in newsletters and public search pages. For example, Upwork generates landing pages containing selections of high-ranking freelancers; these pages are designed to match search engine queries like "medical editor." Some platforms offer talent-recommendation services as an add-on for clients. Overall, the platforms give you access to a large pool of clients from around the world, many of whom you would likely not reach through your own marketing.

Invoices and payments are largely handled for you. For hourly contracts, the sites bill the client automatically on a set schedule. For fixed-price contracts, the client is usually billed in advance, and funds are released to the freelancer when the work is complete.[5] Clients pay the platform, and the platform pays you. You know when you'll be paid for each job without having to chase invoices.

Most platforms provide some form of escrow, payment protection, and dispute-resolution services, but the details and protection vary widely.

There can be some privacy protection. For example, US freelancers typically must provide clients with W-9 forms containing their tax identification number (SSN or EIN) so that the client can issue 1099s for tax reporting. Because the platform pays the freelancer, the W-9 is only provided to the platform, not the client.

---

5. Reedsy is the main exception to the pay-in-advance rule; there, a client's payments are made on milestone dates agreed on between the freelancer and client.

Cons

You must pay fees to the platform. Fees can go as high as 20 percent of the amount billed, which dwarfs payment-processing fees incurred with services like Stripe and PayPal. I'll talk more about fee structures in the next section.

Communication tools may be restricted. Many sites require that all communication between freelancers and clients be done using the platform's tools. Upwork and Guru are exceptions; Upwork requires communication be on the site only until the first contract with a client is started, and Guru doesn't place restrictions.

There are exclusivity rules. The terms of service require that freelancer–client relationships that start on the platform stay on the platform for some time or even forever. Upwork is the only one of these major sites that specifies a time limit: two years. The other sites do not specify a limit to the exclusivity, which, combined with the communication restrictions, can imply that it is indefinite.

You may have privacy concerns. Some platforms, like Upwork and Freelancer.com, use time trackers for hourly jobs. These take screenshots as proof that you are working on the client's project while you are charging time to it. Communication using the site's tools can be monitored by the platform's staff. Summaries of completed projects, including pricing in some cases, are often visible on the freelancer's profile.

You have a lot of competition. These platforms are often swamped with freelancers, making it hard to get noticed and hired, especially as a newcomer.

You may be exposed to scams. As I mentioned in the introduction, freelance platforms provide scammers with a large barrel of potential victims. Freelancers new to a platform are especially at risk. I'll talk more about scams in section 7.

USING FREELANCE PLATFORMS SAFELY AND EFFECTIVELY

How do you choose?

With all these options, how do you choose which platforms to use (if any)? For job boards, review the posted jobs in your field and niche. Are there enough to be worth your time and effort? If there is a freelancer directory or a project board, search the profiles or gigs of other freelancers doing the same type of work. Are people finding success?[6] Of those, do their rates look reasonable to you?

If you've made it past those filters, the next part is more time-consuming: Review how the platform works. Are you comfortable with the business model? Can you work within their rules? Can you live with their fees? The next section will note specifics to look for in your research.

---

6. As long as some freelancers are successful, don't worry too much if many aren't; it can be hard to get started, and many don't find a successful path or give up. If no one is successful in your field or niche, it may mean the client base isn't there, or you may be blazing a new trail.

3. Understanding How a Platform Works

Once you've found a potential platform, it's time to do some research to understand how it works. Many problems discussed in the Upwork forums, for example, start out with the freelancer not understanding how contracts, time tracking, escrow, payment schedules, etc. work there. Jumping into the job feeds without doing basic research is a surefire way to have a bad experience.

First, read the FAQs, help files, and educational material posted on the platform's site. Then, read the entire terms of service (TOS). Your revenue stream will depend on how well you understand the platform's rules, and the best source of those are the TOS.

Find the forums—not just the official ones, but also the unofficial ones, like on Reddit and Facebook. What are people talking about and complaining about? If you have questions on anything you research, chances are someone has already asked that same question in the forums.

Below are some questions to consider. I'll give some examples, but do your own research, especially as platforms may change their terms.

What kind of communication is allowed?

Do you have to use the site's tools to communicate with clients, or can you talk off the platform, such as through email, phone, or Zoom? Most platforms require that you communicate only through their site and that you don't share contact information like email addresses, WhatsApp numbers, etc. As previously noted, Upwork is an exception, as it allows communication any way you want after you and a client start your first contract.[7]

What are the exclusivity rules?

Can you move future work with a client off the platform? In most cases, the TOS explicitly state or imply that all future contracts (and their payments) with a client initially connected with on their site have to stay on the site. Reedsy imposes a fee of at least £4,000 (in Aug. 2021, at least $5,500) for moving a relationship off the platform. Upwork is the only one for which I could find a time limit on the exclusivity: You can move a client's future contracts and payments off the platform two years after you first make contact (e.g., by a client messaging you or you responding to a job post) with that client on Upwork. Before then, they charge a substantial fee based on your annual full-time earnings. Circumventing a platform's exclusivity rule is a ground for suspension or banning.

How do you bid on a job?

The bidding process isn't something you necessarily need to know before joining a job board, but you need to understand it before you start bidding. All job boards have some kind of token used for bidding: Upwork uses "connects," Guru uses "bids," and PeoplePerHour uses "proposal credits." Typically, you get some tokens for free each month, and you can purchase more when you run out.

You'll also want to understand when and how you can ask the client questions. Freelancer.com and Guru have a Q&A board for every

---

7. This is an example of how the rules change. Until June 2020, off-platform communication was allowed on Upwork with no restrictions. The details of the new rule and the exceptions to it have evolved since then.

USING FREELANCE PLATFORMS SAFELY AND EFFECTIVELY

job post where you can ask questions before bidding. On Upwork, you can't communicate with the client about a posted job until they respond to your bid by starting an interview. Guru allows freelancers on certain subscription plans to directly message clients about a job before bidding.

What types of pricing models are supported?

All platforms offer some flavor of **fixed-price contracts**, often with the ability to create intermediate milestone deliveries and payments. Prepackaged projects from project boards, like Fiverr, are fixed-price contracts. Some sites also offer **hourly contracts**, usually with a time tracker that captures regular screenshots of your desktop to show that you're working on the client's project and as documentation in case of disputes. In some cases, you can enter time manually, but that may not qualify for the site's payment protection. Both Upwork and Guru also offer forms of **retainer or salary arrangements**.

Freelancer.com offers **contests**; clients post an open call for entries and then award payment to the chosen freelancer. To submit an entry, freelancers do the work on spec with no guarantee of payment. Contests are most often used for design work, like logos, but there are editing contests as well. Freelancer.com also offers a variation on the project board, which they call "service providers." The platform creates predefined services at set prices and delivery timeframes, such as "proofread up to 1,000 words for $10 in two days." Freelancers can sign up to provide these services but must agree to the price, scope, and deadline that the site has defined. When a client purchases one of these services, the site awards the contract to one of the freelancers registered for it.

What are the fee structures?

Fees can be the biggest surprise for someone jumping in headfirst. All platforms take a portion of project payments—this is how they make their money. The fees go as high as 20 percent, though some offer sliding scales based on either the freelancer's subscription plan level or their lifetime billing with a client. For example, PeoplePerHour's fee starts at 20 percent for the first $350 earned with a client, then drops to 7.5 percent until $7,000 lifetime billing for that client, and then 3.5 percent after that. Upwork has a similar structure. Guru's fee starts at 9 percent and drops as low as 5 percent with more expensive subscription plans.

In most cases, these fees are taken from the client's payment before the money is passed on to the freelancer. Reedsy splits the fees, charging the client 10 percent more than the agreed payment and taking another 10 percent of the payment before sending the rest to the freelancer. Reedsy's fee can drop to as low as 14 percent based on lifetime billing with a client. Freelancer.com's fee on fixed-price contracts is 10 percent, but it's paid by the freelancer when the contract is awarded, before any work is done or any payment is received from the client.

With fee structures like Upwork and PeoplePerHour have, a freelancer can lower their average fees by focusing on clients who are likely to have higher lifetime billing. With structures like Guru's, a freelancer's average fees can be reduced by buying more expensive subscription plans when the freelancer's monthly billing becomes large enough to justify the additional plan cost. Some freelancers choose to pass the platform fees on to their client by increasing their prices to offset the fees.

There are other fees as well. On some job boards, you can buy upgrades to highlight your bids in the (often lengthy) list presented to clients, move them to the top of the client's queue, or, on Freelancer.com, seal your bid so that other freelancers can't view your quote and cover letter. It also costs to bid on jobs after you've exhausted your free bids. Most platforms have monthly subscription packages that offer perks, extra features, and additional bid tokens to freelancers.

There are also payment-processing fees, usually paid by the client, but at Reedsy, they are paid by the freelancer. There can be withdrawal fees, which I cover below, depending on how you move your money from the platform.

Some good news: At tax time, these fees may be deductible as a business expense; talk to your tax professional about this.

USING FREELANCE PLATFORMS SAFELY AND EFFECTIVELY

How do you get a contract?

It's important to know how the contract process works, how to verify that you actually have a contract, and where in the process you have a chance to vet the client and their material. A common mistake people make on their first job is hearing the client say, "you're hired," doing the work, and turning it over without ever setting up a contract. Without the contract, there's no way to get paid.

On job boards and freelancer directories, the process usually involves an interview between the freelancer and client to agree on terms; one party then creates a contract offer through the site, which the other accepts. The interview is often the best time to vet the client, as the discussion can reveal red flags and may give you additional information about the client to research on Google and LinkedIn.

On project boards, like Fiverr, it's common for contracts to be created automatically when the client places an order, without the freelancer's involvement. This can make vetting a challenge, so you need to know whether there's a period during which you can get out of the contract without any penalty or effect on your ratings. Because you aren't involved in taking orders, you will need to know how to limit the number of them you can receive at a time so that you don't get overloaded. This will usually be a setting you can adjust on the project listing.

How do you get paid?

At some point in the contract, the client pays the platform; after that, the money—minus fees—lands in your account there. Many platforms have some form of escrow system for fixed-price projects; the client pays up front and the platform holds the money until the client approves your work. There can also be security periods that, in essence, give the client's payment a chance to clear.

Understanding how the escrow process works and how to get money released from escrow is critical if you're doing fixed-price projects. For example, on Upwork, a client funds either the entire project or the first milestone up front; Upwork holds that money in escrow. When the work for that payment is complete, the freelancer must click a "submit work" button on the contract, even if the work is handed over through another path, like email, Google Drive, or Dropbox. The client approves the work by clicking another button, which releases the payment. There's also an option for the client to ask for revisions. If the client doesn't approve the work or ask for revisions within two weeks of the freelancer submitting it, the money is automatically released from escrow to the freelancer. This is part of the payment protection the platform offers freelancers. Guru's variation is the optional SafePay account, which is shared between the client and the freelancer but isn't tied to any specific project. The freelancer can specify what portion of a project has to be funded in the account, and the client releases payment for milestones or projects from there.

Once payments land in your account on the platform, how do you get that money to someplace where it's usable, like PayPal or your bank? There are usually a few different transfer methods, some of which may have fees assessed by either the platform or the receiving end. For example, for payment to US freelancers, Upwork offers an ACH transfer to your bank for free but will charge $1 for each transfer to a PayPal account. On Fiverr, these charges are flipped: Transfers to PayPal are free, but ACH transfers cost $1 each.

What currency will you be paid in? If it isn't your currency, you may need to consider conversion fees. Some sites offer multiple currencies; for example, PeoplePerHour pays in dollars, euros, or pounds.

How do the freelancer ratings work?

All of these platforms display reviews from clients and use some form of the five-star rating system. In most cases, these are the most prominently displayed statistics, but there are others that may either be visible to the client or used behind the scenes to rank freelancers. Upwork displays the five-star rating on individual public reviews clients give freelancers. As a summary metric, the platform shows an aggregated Job Success Score

USING FREELANCE PLATFORMS SAFELY AND EFFECTIVELY

(JSS) based largely on a 10-point "private feedback" score[8] given by clients rather than showing a freelancer's average five-star rating. Freelancers never see individual private-feedback scores; instead, a freelancer sees an aggregate percentage score labeled "clients who would recommend you." Freelancer.com shows clients several freelancer statistics, such as jobs completed, delivered on time, and delivered on budget and the freelancer's repeat-hire rate. Some platforms, like Upwork and Reedsy, also display a responsiveness rating based on how quickly you respond to clients' first messages.

What is the dispute process?

Most platforms have some mechanism to help freelancers and clients resolve contract and payment disputes. Hopefully, you never have to use this service, and you don't really need to know the full details of the process until you need it. But you should know whether the platform will get in the middle of disputes and where you can find the process if you ever need it. Details are usually included in the TOS.

Summary

As you research platforms, write down other questions that come up for you. If you can't find answers in the TOS, FAQ, or educational materials, you can often find them in the forums.

---

8. This is similar to the Net Promoter Score (NPS) used by many businesses to track customer satisfaction.

4. Establishing and Managing Your Reputation

Reputation is everything on the freelance platforms. When you work directly with clients, you can choose which testimonials to share as part of your marketing. On freelance platforms, clients' reviews of your service and the summary ratings based on those reviews are highly visible to prospects deciding whether to hire you or even interview you. You have little, if any, control over those reviews and ratings other than through your service quality.

Once you have a solid reputation, meaning you've successfully completed several jobs and have a collection of good reviews on your profile, you will stand out more in searches and your bids will make more of an impression. You'll be better able to command the rates you want. The feedback and scores on your profile do much of the selling for you.

Building a reputation takes time and patience. It takes completing jobs successfully and getting consistently positive feedback from clients. On the job boards, it can also take a lot of bidding tokens, which translates to money. Without a job history and good feedback scores, landing projects is much like pitching clients directly: You have to sell yourself through your profile and your bids or packaged-project descriptions.

Writing winning profiles and proposals is a large topic in itself. A wealth of good information on these topics is available, including in other EFA booklets and courses, and most platforms have site-specific tips in their educational material. Don't forget to look at other successful freelancers' profiles for inspiration. Certainly don't copy them, but look at the information they provide and the structure they use. See what works and how you can apply that for your own profile.

Building a reputation isn't enough. You need to manage that reputation, especially at first. A poor review early on is much more harmful than one after you have pages of five-star reviews. Be selective in what you take on, especially at first. Take jobs you know you can deliver well. Taking risks with projects that push your skill set is fine once you have a great feedback history to offset a miss, but be very wary of doing so at first. Also consider whether you want a particular job showing on your job history. If you are positioning yourself as a nonfiction book editor, for example, do you want prospective clients to see that you're taking screen scraping or data entry work?[9]

Being selective also involves vetting clients, which I'll talk more about in section 6. Look at a client's review history, if available on the platform[10]—both the reviews they've received and those they've given. If a client has a history of giving freelancers poor reviews, don't take the chance that they'll treat you any differently.

Finally, some platforms allow freelancers to respond publicly to clients' reviews. Be very careful doing so. An angry response to a bad review looks unprofessional and can leave a worse impression on a prospective client than the original review. It will also draw more attention to a review that will hopefully soon be buried by good ones.

---

9. There's nothing wrong with this type of work, but the jobs may give the impression you're not successful in or serious about your advertised field.

10. On Upwork, for example, reviews are visible on clients' job posts.

5. Setting Rates

It can be difficult to know where to set your rates. This topic is extensively discussed elsewhere, so I won't go into detail about determining your base rates. Two good starting points are EFA's Editorial Rates Survey, last refreshed in 2020, and their recorded webinars on the subject. In this section, I'll talk about some aspects of rates specific to the freelance platforms.

There are a couple of guideposts you can use. Just as when you're setting up your profile, you can browse other freelancers' profiles in your field and niche to see what they're charging. If the platform shows pricing details in freelancers' job histories, you can also scroll back to see how their pricing evolved with their experience.

Also consider the site's search filters. For example, Upwork's freelancer search has an hourly rate filter with options for "Any rate," "$10 and below," "$10 to $30," "$30 to $60," and "$60 and above."[11] Certainly not all clients use those search filters, but some do, and when you move your rates from one band to another, you affect which clients will see your profile.

As I mentioned in the last section, it can be hard to get a foothold in these marketplaces. One technique to widen your prospect pool as you get started is to slightly discount your rate to attract the more price-sensitive clients. As you build your reputation on the platform, you can gradually raise your rate back to where you want it to be—and then

---

11. You might be asking if a $10, $30, or $60 rate will show in two search categories. The answer is no—the ranges should say "$10.01 to $30," etc.

higher. Just as when working with clients directly, the timing of increases can be a balancing act between having too much work at a lower rate and not enough at a higher one.

If you do discount your rates, be careful of going below professional rates. In active freelance marketplaces, competing solely on price is a losing game—there will always be someone willing to bid lower than you. Some people point to this as evidence of a "race to the bottom," where the going rate for a service keeps dropping. However, I see (loosely speaking) two markets.

Some clients see the freelance platforms as a source of cheap work; they exploit freelancers, especially new ones, who feel they must accept any rate to get work and build their reputation. Based on complaints in freelancer forums, these can also be the most difficult clients to work with, and they often look for excuses to not pay the already low rates.

Other clients on the platforms know the value of professional work and will pay for it. There is certainly price variation and sensitivity at this level, but it's not as extreme as in the overall marketplace. With these clients, quality, service, and price are all important.

Clients in the first category, the low end, are unlikely to hire freelancers who price for the second set, and vice versa. There is little competition between the two groups. As a freelancer, you can choose which of these (again, loosely defined) groups you want to serve. Set your rates and ignore clients paying significantly below them.

6. Vetting Clients and Their Material

One of the most important tasks when using freelance platforms is to vet your clients and their material as much as possible. This helps you build and maintain your reputation, avoid scams, and avoid getting stuck with an underpriced project because of a scope misunderstanding. Some of these considerations are no different than when finding clients directly, but there are aspects specific to the platforms, and some platforms and business models make vetting easier than others.

Do not assume that a platform has vetted any client. At most, they will do some simple verification to make sure that the client's payment method is valid and, in some cases, that the client has given a valid email and phone number. A scammer or otherwise unscrupulous client can easily work around those checks.

On the job boards, you will usually have access to a client's name at some point in the bidding and interview process (though this may be a business name, or it may not be the client's full name or even real name). In the job post itself, the name will probably be abbreviated. Once an interview has started, you may have access to additional details, including their full name and possibly their organization's name. If the material isn't attached to the job post, you can (and should) ask to see it as part of the interview.

If you have enough information, you can check LinkedIn, the client's company or institution web pages, and Google to see if the client looks legitimate. Finding matches this way doesn't necessarily mean they are who they say they are—some scammers will fake this information—but it increases the odds that they are a legitimate client. More importantly, if you don't find information that you think you should, that can be a red flag.

If you have access to the client's review history, look at how other freelancers reviewed them and how they reviewed other freelancers. Seeing freelancers' reviews of a client can help you avoid someone who is difficult to work with, moves the goalposts, or avoids payment. If you see a client who consistently gives poor reviews, it's a safe bet they are difficult to please. In both cases, consider the percentage of good versus bad reviews. An unhappy experience is bound to happen eventually, but patterns can point to problems that are best avoided.

Assuming the client has passed your vetting, also vet their material before you give a firm quote or accept the contract. Never assume what the client has told you about the material is true. Both on and off freelance platforms, clients can misrepresent the amount of work needed and the quality of what they are giving you. In most cases, this probably isn't malicious; it may just be inexperience. Clients often don't use the same terms as professionals. For example, "proofreading" is often used as a generic term for anything editors do (and many things they don't), including copyediting, content writing, plagiarism mitigation, book design, and translation (yes, really). Word counts can be very loosely estimated, and text that has been "very well edited and just needs a quick second look before I publish it" can turn out to have been drunktated to Siri or run through Google Translate with no cleanup. Reviewing the material before accepting the contract can avoid these issues. You should also make sure that the material is something that you're comfortable working with.

On the project boards, such vetting may not be possible before the contract begins. In this model, the default is for the client to order a project with a predefined scope, thereby starting the contract. The client then delivers the material. At this point, your vetting can start. If you find red flags or the delivered material is outside the package's predefined scope, you may have limited time to cancel the contract, and you may need to involve customer support to avoid such cancellations from impacting your statistics.

7. Avoiding Scams

The most common complaint I hear about freelance platforms is the prevalence of scams perpetrated from both the freelancer and client sides. I assume the freelancers reading this booklet are honest professionals, so I'm just going to talk about the client side. One thing that makes scams easier to pull off on platforms is that when a freelancer has zero or limited job history and reviews, they stand out as newcomers. They may not have taken the time to learn how the platform works (section 3). Unfortunately, these new freelancers are scam magnets. You're less of a target when your job history builds up. I'll start off by describing several common scams, and then I'll talk about how to avoid them in general.

Common scams

Bogus check: The client will say you need some special equipment, like a computer, to work on their project. They'll send you a check, or payment via the platform, and ask you to use the money to buy the equipment, presumably from a storefront they own. Once the bank or platform determines the payment is fake, it will take the money out of your account. If you've already paid for the equipment (which will never arrive), you're out of luck. Accepting a check may also violate the platform's payment rules, putting your account at risk of suspension. Variations on this scam ask you to buy gift cards, Google Play credits, Steam credits, etc. and send them to the scammer.

Identify theft: The scammer asks for personal information, saying it's required for the job application or to get a company credit card, which will somehow be required for the job. With a few details, they have enough information to get credit in your name.

Buying or leasing your platform account: Scammers will say they can't get a platform account in their own name for some reason, like it's not allowed in their country or they've been unjustly banned. These are likely people who either were not accepted on the platform or who have been banned for fraud or breaking the rules. They will offer to pay you for your account, possibly with monthly "lease" payments. If you agree, you'll have to give them your username and password, which gives them access to your personal details, enabling identity theft, and the ability to change where your payments are sent. When they scam clients or turn in shoddy work using your account, the resulting bad reviews will trash your reputation on the platform. In addition, any income they earn is in your name, leaving you responsible for refunds and taxes.

Feedback blackmail: Playing on fears of bad reviews, unscrupulous clients will move the goalposts, continually adding more scope for no extra pay. If you balk, they threaten to leave a bad review. Avoiding the bottom-of-the-barrel jobs in terms of pay will keep you away from most of these jobs, but if you find yourself stuck, the best option is usually to end the contract and report the client to the platform. If you can prove you were blackmailed, the platform may remove any feedback the client left.

Promising more work later at better pay: A common recruiting tactic is to offer a low rate as a trial with the promise to raise it with the next job. Spoiler alert: It probably won't be raised. This scam can go hand in hand with feedback blackmail.

Use your address to register a foreign business: In this scam, you are asked to register the client's business with Google or some other site using your physical address so the business appears to be in your country rather than theirs. If you agree, you now have their future scams tied to your address.

Refusing to pay: As I mentioned earlier, some clients who look to freelance platforms as source of cheap work also look for free work by making up excuses to not pay or by demanding a refund. Common claims are that there are defects, that deadlines are missed, and that the work was plagiarized. Again, this will often involve feedback blackmail. Following the platform's guidelines for turning over and documenting work will help you with disputes like this. The platform's payment-protection and dispute policies depend on you being able to show you've done the work you were hired to do.

Avoiding scams

To avoid scams, pay attention and use common sense. Here are some common red flags:

- Is the job unrelated to the services you're offering?
- Would a reasonable person make this offer, like sending money to buy equipment, to someone they haven't met or worked with before? Would you make that offer?
- Are you making yourself legally or financially responsible for something the client should take care of?
- Are they asking you to bypass the site's safeguards and policies, like the payment and communication rules? It's common for scammers to try to get the freelancer to "interview" outside of the platform's channels. Often this interview is with a "hiring manager." If you agree to an off-platform interview, the platform has no record of the scam's details, and you've put yourself at risk of being banned for communicating outside the platform.
- Have they contacted you with an unsolicited offer even though you have no (or limited) job history so far? Legitimate clients often make unsolicited offers to freelancers with a proven track record. For newcomers, it's very likely the start of a scam.
- Are they asking for personal information they don't need? They could just be confused; some clients believe they need tax forms that the platforms take care of. Or they could be trying to steal your

identity. In some cases, some personal information is necessary, such as your name and business address for a nondisclosure agreement (NDA),[12] but be careful about providing more.
- Are they saying they've paid the site's fee to hire you off the platform (like Upwork's Conversion Fee or Reedsy's Introduction Fee)? These run several thousand dollars and are unlikely to be paid by a client you haven't worked with extensively.

If you're unsure about a situation, post in the site's forums to ask if others see an issue, or search the forums to see if others have reported the same thing. It's cheaper to learn from another's mistake than to make it yourself.

- Don't assume the platform has vetted the client. It has not.
- Don't assume the platform will protect you from scams. It won't.
- And don't assume the platform will reimburse you or help you recover anything you've lost in a scam. It won't.
- Most importantly, trust your gut. If the situation feels off, it probably is.

---

12. Some platforms, like Freelancer.com and PeoplePerHour, offer built-in processes (for an extra fee) for handling NDAs. Others, like Upwork, leave those to the client and freelancer to work out. Upwork currently makes an exception to their contact-detail rule for NDAs.

8. Parting Words

Before I go, I want to share a few final tips.

Don't put all your eggs in one basket. Some platforms are quick to suspend or ban freelancers for infractions, even suspected ones. Platforms can go out of business or fall out of favor. Consider diversifying across platforms or between one platform and direct-billed clients. If you're just starting out, this may seem like too much at once, but you can make it part of your long-term plan and work toward it.

Don't wait for responses to bids. After you send off a bid, keep looking for other jobs that are a good fit. You can worry about scheduling conflicts when clients respond. Response rates, especially at first, can be low. Even after a client's initial response to a bid, don't consider a time slot sold until it's clear they're going to move forward with an offer, as prospective clients may simply ghost you without ever saying they've selected someone else (or no one at all).

Be patient and persistent. It can take a long time to get the first job. And the second. And the third. But as your profile history builds, it gets easier. The majority of people registered on these platforms never get their first job, let alone their second. But these people aren't you, are they?

Good luck!

References

General

Editorial Freelancers Association. "Editorial Rates." Accessed May 22, 2021. https://www.the-efa.org/rates/.

FDIC Consumer News. "Beware of Fake Checks." Accessed May 25, 2021. https://www.fdic.gov/consumers/consumer/news/august2019.html.

Hutchinson, Andrew. "LinkedIn's Developing a New Freelance Marketplace Platform to Facilitate New Opportunities." *Social Media Today*, February 29, 2021. https://www.socialmediatoday.com/news/linkedins-developing-a-new-freelance-marketplace-platform-to-facilitate-ne/595397/.

Payoneer. "Fees." Accessed May 20, 2021. https://www.payoneer.com/about/fees/.

PayPal. "What Are the Fees for PayPal Accounts?" Accessed May 20, 2021. https://www.paypal.com/us/smarthelp/article/what-are-the-fees-for-paypal-accounts-faq690.

Fiverr

Fiverr.com. "Achieving Levels." Accessed May 21, 2021. https://www.fiverr.com/support/articles/360010925137-Levels-Statistics?segment=seller.

Fiverr.com. "Chargebacks and Seller Protection."
Accessed May 18, 2021.
https://www.fiverr.com/support/
articles/360010978618-Chargebacks-and-seller-protection.

Fiverr. "Fiverr Announces First Quarter 2021 Results," 2021.
https://investors.fiverr.com/press-releases/press-releases-details/2021/
Fiverr-Announces-First-Quarter-2021-Results/default.aspx.

Fiverr.com. "Fiverr's Terms of Service." Accessed May 16, 2021.
https://www.fiverr.com/terms_of_service.

Fiverr.com. "How Do I Find a Service and Get a Quote?"
Accessed May 23, 2021.
https://www.fiverr.com/support/
articles/360010451297-How-to-Start-Selling-on-Fiverr.

Fiverr.com. "How Fiverr Works." Accessed May 18, 2021.
https://www.fiverr.com/support/
articles/360010558038-How-Fiverr-Works?segment=buyer.

Fiverr.com. "Levels Statistics." Accessed May 21, 2021.
https://www.fiverr.com/support/
articles/360010925137-Levels-Statistics?segment=seller.

Fiverr.com. "Limiting Orders in Queue." Accessed May 21, 2021.
https://www.fiverr.com/support/
articles/360010925137-Levels-Statistics?segment=seller.

Fiverr.com. "Order Completion Rate and Cancellations FAQ."
Accessed May 23, 2021.
https://www.fiverr.com/support/
articles/360010451297-How-to-Start-Selling-on-Fiverr.

Fiverr.com. "Payments Terms and Conditions." Accessed May 16, 2021.
https://www.fiverr.com/content/payments-terms-and-conditions.

Fiverr.com. "Response Time & Rate FAQ." Accessed May 21, 2021.
https://www.fiverr.com/support/
articles/360010925137-Levels-Statistics?segment=seller.

u/FionaAudronVO. "[ADVICE] If You Have Something Listed in Your Profile That You Don't Do (That Would Be Typical of Your Job) Does CS Take Your Side in Disputes?" r/Fiverr, Reddit, May 9, 2021. https://www.reddit.com/r/Fiverr/comments/n8mptq/advice_if_you_have_something_listed_in_your/.

u/msannan121. "[HELP] Someone Placed an Order One Week Ago and Still Hasn't Given Any Requirements." r/Fiverr, Reddit, June 3, 2021. www.reddit.com/r/Fiverr/comments/nrovu6/help_someone_placed_an_order_one_week_ago_and/.

Freelancer.com

Freelancer. "2020 Annual Report," 2020. https://www.freelancer.com/about/investor-pdf.php?id=140904784&name=ANNUAL%20REPORT%202020%20FINAL%20Compressed.

Freelancer. "Bidding on Projects." Accessed May 21, 2021. https://www.freelancer.com/support/freelancer/Project/how-to-bid-1633.

Freelancer. "Browse: Contests." Accessed July 9, 2021. https://www.freelancer.com/search/contests.

Freelancer. "Browse: Freelancers." Accessed July 9, 2021. https://www.freelancer.com/search/users.

Freelancer. "Browse: Projects." Accessed July 9, 2021. https://www.freelancer.com/search/projects.

Freelancer. "Choosing the Right Freelancer." Accessed May 23, 2021. https://www.freelancer.com/support/employer/Project/how-to-select-the-right-bidder.

Freelancer. "Desktop Application." Accessed May 21, 2021. https://www.freelancer.com/desktop-app/.

Freelancer. "Financial Dashboard." Accessed May 18, 2021. https://www.freelancer.com/support/payments/financial-dashboard.

Freelancer. "Freelancer Contests." Accessed May 21, 2021. https://www.freelancer.com/contest/.

Freelancer. "Freelancer Fees and Charges." Accessed May 15, 2021. https://www.freelancer.com/feesandcharges.

Freelancer. "Freelancer Membership Plans." Accessed May 15, 2021. https://www.freelancer.com/membership.

Freelancer. "Freelancer Services." Accessed May 15, 2021. https://www.freelancer.com/support/general/freelancer-services.

Freelancer. "Freelancer Services: Proofread an Article." Accessed June 6, 2021. https://www.freelancer.com/services/Proofread-an-article-56759.html.

Freelancer. "Job Completion Rate." Accessed May 18, 2021. https://www.freelancer.com/support/freelancer/Project/what-is-the-completion-rate.

Freelancer. "Milestone Payments." Accessed May 18, 2021. https://www.freelancer.com/support/freelancer/Payments/milestone-payment-for-employers-2228.

Freelancer. "User Agreement." Accessed May 15, 2021. https://www.freelancer.com/about/terms.

Freelancer. "Welcome to Freelancer Services," March 23, 2017. https://www.freelancer.com/community/articles/welcome-to-freelancer-services.

Guru

Guru. "About SafePay." Accessed May 18, 2021. https://www.guru.com/help/freelancer/about-safepay-freelancer/.

Guru. "Benefits of Paid Membership." Accessed May 15, 2021. https://www.guru.com/pricing-freelancer/.

Guru. "Find and Hire Freelancers." Accessed July 9, 2021. https://www.guru.com/d/freelancers/.

Guru. "Find Freelance Jobs." Accessed July 9, 2021. https://www.guru.com/d/jobs/.

Guru. "Hiring a Freelancer," December 27, 2019. https://www.guru.com/help/employer/hiring-a-freelancer/.

Guru. "Job Q&A." Accessed May 15, 2021. https://www.guru.com/help/freelancer/job-qa-freelancer/.

Guru. "Payment Terms." Accessed May 18, 2021. https://www.guru.com/help/freelancer/payment-terms-freelancer/.

Guru. "Pricing for Employers." Accessed May 15, 2021. https://www.guru.com/pricing-employer/.

Guru. "Purchase Bids." Accessed May 15, 2021. https://www.guru.com/help/freelancer/purchase-bids/.

Guru. "Payment Protection with SafePay." Accessed May 18, 2021. https://www.guru.com/safepay/.

Guru. "Sales Messages." Accessed May 15, 2021. https://www.guru.com/help/freelancer/sales-messages/.

Guru. "Terms of Service." Accessed May 15, 2021. https://www.guru.com/terms-of-service/.

Jones, Cory. "6 Tips on Communicating with Employers on Guru." *Guru* (blog), June 11, 2013. https://www.guru.com/blog/6-tips-communicating-employers/.

PeoplePerHour

PeoplePerHour. "About PeoplePerHour." Accessed July 9, 2021.
https://www.peopleperhour.com/about.

PeoplePerHour. "Freelance Projects." Accessed July 9, 2021.
https://www.peopleperhour.com/freelance-jobs.

PeoplePerHour. "Freelancer Commission Fees."
Accessed May 16, 2021.
https://support.peopleperhour.com/hc/en-us/articles/205218337-Freelancer-commission-fees.

PeoplePerHour. "Freelancer Should Be Given Option to Initiate Cancellation a Project with Full Refund without Penalty." Accessed May 23, 2021.
http://support.peopleperhour.com/hc/en-us/community/posts/360011761297-Freelancer-Should-be-Given-Option-to-Initiate-Cancellation-a-Project-with-Full-Refund-without-Penalty.

PeoplePerHour. "Job Deposits and Minimum Proposal Amounts." Accessed May 23, 2021.
https://support.peopleperhour.com/hc/en-us/articles/205217997-Job-Deposits-and-minimum-Proposal-amounts.

PeoplePerHour. "Offers Add-Ons." Accessed May 23, 2021.
https://support.peopleperhour.com/hc/en-us/articles/205218037-Offers-Add-ons.

PeoplePerHour. "Posting Offers." Accessed May 23, 2021.
https://support.peopleperhour.com/hc/en-us/articles/205217517-Posting-Offers.

PeoplePerHour. "Rules of Engagement." Accessed May 23, 2021.
https://support.peopleperhour.com/hc/en-us/articles/205217317-Rules-of-Engagement.

PeoplePerHour. "Terms and Conditions." Accessed May 16, 2021.
https://www.peopleperhour.com/static/terms.

PeoplePerHour. "The Basics." Accessed May 23, 2021. https://support.peopleperhour.com/hc/en-us/articles/205217187-The-Basics.

PeoplePerHour. "Understanding the Escrow." Accessed May 18, 2021. https://support.peopleperhour.com/hc/en-us/articles/205217777-Understanding-the-Escrow.

Reedsy

Reedsy. "Can I Cancel My Collaboration?" Accessed May 23, 2021. https://reedsy.crisp.help/en-us/article/can-i-cancel-my-collaboration-11915yn/.

Reedsy. "How Can I Structure My Fees?" Accessed May 20, 2021. https://reedsy.crisp.help/en-us/article/how-can-i-structure-my-fees-3qva1q/.

Reedsy. "How Does Contracting Work on Reedsy?" Accessed May 23, 2021. https://reedsy.crisp.help/en-us/article/how-does-contracting-work-on-reedsy-yurdkc/.

Reedsy. "How Does My Response Rate Work?" Accessed May 23, 2021. https://reedsy.crisp.help/en-us/article/how-does-my-response-rate-work-ij9nnq/.

Reedsy. "How Much Does Reedsy Cost?" Accessed May 16, 2021. https://reedsy.crisp.help/en-us/article/how-much-does-reedsy-cost-1sfno8v/.

Reedsy. "Terms of Use." Accessed May 16, 2021. https://reedsy.com/about/tou.

Reedsy. "We Are Reedsy!" Accessed July 9, 2021. https://reedsy.com/about.

Reedsy. "Why Should I Pay and Communicate Only through Reedsy?" Accessed May 23, 2021.
https://reedsy.crisp.help/en-us/article/
why-should-i-pay-and-communicate-only-through-reedsy-sn28io/.

Upwork

Upwork. "Annual Report 2020," 2020.
https://investors.upwork.com/
static-files/3e32780b-95da-429b-9f36-22b5e508d6f7.

Upwork. "Client Payment Processing Fees." Accessed May 15, 2021.
https://support.upwork.com/hc/en-us/
articles/218375638-Client-Payment-Processing-Fees.

Upwork. "Communicating On and Outside of Upwork — Terms of Service Changes," May 26, 2020.
https://community.upwork.com/t5/Announcements/
Communicating-On-and-Outside-of-Upwork-Terms-of-Service-Changes/m-p/753812#M42429.

Upwork. "Connects: Upwork's Virtual Currency." Accessed May 15, 2021.
https://support.upwork.com/hc/en-us/
articles/211062898-Connects-Upwork-s-Virtual-Currency.

Upwork. "Create a Project." Accessed May 23, 2021.
https://support.upwork.com/hc/en-us/
articles/360057397533-Create-a-Project.

Upwork. "Featured Jobs." Accessed May 15, 2021.
https://support.upwork.com/hc/en-us/
articles/115010165067-Featured-Jobs.

Upwork. "Freelance Jobs." Accessed July 9, 2021.
https://www.upwork.com/ab/jobs/
search/?sort=recency&user_location_match=2.

USING FREELANCE PLATFORMS SAFELY AND EFFECTIVELY

Upwork. "Freelancer Plus." Accessed May 15, 2021. https://support.upwork.com/hc/en-us/articles/211062888-Freelancer-Plus.

Upwork. "Freelancer Search Results." Accessed May 22, 2021. https://www.upwork.com/ab/profiles/search/.

Upwork. "Freelancer Service Fees." Accessed May 15, 2021. https://support.upwork.com/hc/en-us/articles/211062538-Freelancer-Service-Fees.

Upwork. "Investor Day." June 2021. https://upwork.gcs-web.com/static-files/11fe6ce1-8c50-40e5-9f4e-2710de4e27c8.

Upwork. "Move Outside of Upwork." Accessed May 18, 2021. https://support.upwork.com/hc/en-us/articles/360043210654-Move-Outside-of-Upwork.

Upwork. "Pay for Hourly Contracts." Accessed May 21, 2021. https://support.upwork.com/hc/en-us/articles/211067938-Pay-for-Hourly-Contracts.

Upwork. "Sharing Information on Upwork." Accessed May 15, 2021. https://support.upwork.com/hc/en-us/articles/360049608113-Sharing-Information-on-Upwork.

Upwork. "Upwork Plus." Accessed May 15, 2021. https://support.upwork.com/hc/en-us/articles/360018800733-Upwork-Plus.

About the
Editorial Freelancers Association (EFA)

Celebrating 50 Years!
Dedicated to the Education and Growth
of Editorial Freelancers

The EFA is a national not-for-profit — 501(c)6 — organization, headquartered in New York City, run by member volunteers, all of whom are also freelancers. The EFA's members, experienced in a wide range of professional skills, live and work all across the United States and in other countries.

A pioneer in organizing freelancers into a network for mutual support and advancement, the EFA is now recognized throughout the publishing industry as the source for professional editorial assistance.

We welcome people of every race, color, culture, religion or no religion, gender identity, gender expression, age, national or ethnic origin, ancestry, citizenship, education, ability, health, neurotype, marital/parental status, socio-economic background, sexual orientation, and/or military status. We are nothing without our members, and encourage everyone to volunteer and to participate in our community.

The EFA sells a variety of specialized booklets, not unlike this one, on topics of interest to editorial freelancers at the-efa.org.

The EFA hosts online, asynchronous courses, real-time webinars, and on-demand recorded webinars designed especially for freelance editors, writers, and other editorial specialists around the world. You can learn more about our Education Program at the-efa.org.

To learn about these and other EFA offerings, visit the-efa.org and join us on social media:

Twitter: @EFAFreelancers
Instagram: @efa_editors
Facebook: editorialfreelancersassociation
LinkedIn: editorial-freelancers

CPSIA information can be obtained
at www.ICGtesting.com
Printed in the USA
LVHW080331060422
715471LV00016B/204